WRATH OF THE WAVES

Marlatt

AHEAD

CAPTAIN'S ORDERS
in 1 ♩ = 60

SUN OFF THE BOW
Much Slower ♩ = 88

A GOLD TOOTH GRIN

WRATH OF THE WAVES pg. 4

B♭ Trumpet 1

WRATH OF THE WAVES

David Marlatt

Bb Trumpet 2

WRATH OF THE WAVES

David Marlatt

F Horn

WRATH OF THE WAVES

David Marlatt

Trombone

WRATH OF THE WAVES

David Marlatt

Tuba

WRATH OF THE WAVES

David Marlatt

JIG ON DECK

SHIVER ME TIMBERS
With Pulse ♩ = 160